Ancient Magick for
Today's Witch Series

ABUNDANCE SPELLS

MONIQUE JOINER SIEDLAK

OSHUN
PUBLICATIONS
oshunpublications.com

Cover Design by MJS

Cover Images by MidJourney

Published by Oshun Publications

www.oshunpublications.com

Published by Oshun Publications

www.oshunpublications.com

ANCIENT MAGICK FOR TODAY'S WITCH SERIES

The *Ancient Magick for Today's Witch Series* is a series for modern witches to explore ancient magick, covering Celtic, Gypsy, and Crystal magic, among others. It offers practical advice on spells, rituals, and enchantments for today's use, incorporating natural energies and spiritual connections. With insights into Shamanism, Wicca, and more, it helps readers enhance their magickal journey, offering paths to protection, prosperity, and spiritual growth by combining ancient wisdom with contemporary practice.

Wiccan Basics

Candle Magick

Wiccan Spells

Love Spells

Abundance Spells

Herb Magick

Moon Magick

Creating Your Own Spells

Gypsy Magic

Protection Magick

Celtic Magick

Shamanic Magick

Crystal Magic

Sacred Spaces

Solitary Witchcraft

Novice Witch's Guide

MONIQUE JOINER SIEDLAK
GET UPDATES, FREEBIES & GIVEAWAYS
JOIN MY NEWSLETTER
MOJOSIEDLAK.COM/MOONLIGHT-MUSINGS

CONTENTS

Introduction to Abundance Spells   xiii

1. Debt-Banishing Spells   1
2. Aligning Career with Spiritual Purpose   11
3. The Nature of Luck and How to Influence It   27
4. Wealth Magnetism   41
5. Mastering Mindset   65
6. Inner Wealth   73

Conclusion   81
References   87
About the Author   89
More Books by Monique   91
Don't Miss Out   95

INTRODUCTION TO ABUNDANCE SPELLS

You wish to be prosperous, you want abundance, and you have a wonderful purpose in life. You want to do this for your neighborhood, for your household. But you work—always working. You keep struggling, but nevertheless, it doesn't work for you. Frequently, the economic decisions we make are instinctive and based on worry. Since money is extensively linked to our physical survival, it has a significant influence on us and forces us to feel like we can't manage it.

When you claim or frequently think statements such as, "*I can't afford this*" or "*I'll never get ahead in life,*" you're surrounding yourself with a spirit that brings poverty and economic struggle to your world. It's essential to see yourself as successful, blessed, and even wealthy if you wish to genuinely become these things. It's actually the thought of "*Fake it till you make it.*" It's not that you need to fib to others about how much money you make (I share that with only my husband), you need to be positive. Stay focused on what you DO want as opposed to what you don't want.

Abundance Spells illuminates the empowering intersection of financial management and spiritual practices, demonstrating how traditional money-handling techniques can be elevated by incorporating spiritual elements. The intention behind this approach is not only to accumulate wealth, but also to appreciate and respect the energy associated with money. In numerous cultures, money is not merely a medium of exchange but a force that carries its own spiritual significance. When individuals treat money with respect and purpose, they can invite more financial abundance and stability, fostering hope and motivation. This integration inspires you to see the potential for financial growth and stability in your life.

The concept of *Abundance Spells* is rooted in the belief that our financial lives can benefit significantly from a touch of the mystical. These methods cover everything from casting spells in Wiccan tradition for debt relief and attracting wealth, to implementing Feng Shui techniques for promoting prosperity and harmony. Moreover, it extends to the psychological aspects of financial dealings, where mindfulness and positive thinking play crucial roles in maintaining a healthy financial state.

Abundance Spells combines traditional financial planning with spells, rituals, affirmations, and meditative practices for a holistic approach. It emphasizes the importance of aligning one's financial actions with one's spiritual values and goals. Through this unique combination, individuals cannot only enhance their financial well-being but also achieve a deeper sense of satisfaction and personal fulfillment, creating a balanced and prosperous life.

The Connection between Wiccan Spells, Mindsets, and Finance

The integration of Wiccan spells and mindsets into financial management is a powerful testament to how spirituality can influence financial success. In Wicca, a modern pagan religion, the emphasis is on intention and energy in everyday activities, which can be utilized to effectively manage and enhance one's financial well-being. The use of spells—ritualistic practices aimed at manifesting a desired outcome—is pivotal in this approach, instilling a proactive attitude towards financial goals and inspiring the audience.

Wiccan spells centered around finance usually consist of rituals meant to draw in wealth, enhance financial luck, and eliminate debts. These spells often use symbolic materials like herbs, candles, and crystals, each chosen for their supposed properties and correspondences to monetary success. By casting these spells, practitioners can improve their motivation and achieve better outcomes by focusing on their intentions and visualizing their financial goals, as suggested by psychological studies.

In addition, Wiccans embrace a mindset that fosters a positive and respectful relationship with money, recognizing it as an energetic resource that must be circulated responsibly and ethically. This viewpoint promotes a transition from pure acquisition to a more comprehensive resource management approach, where individuals earn and spend money in accordance with their ethical and spiritual convictions.

Incorporating these spiritual practices into financial management is different from traditional financial planning. Still, it enhances it by adding a layer of personal meaning and motivation. By taking a holistic approach, individuals can achieve not just financial prosperity but also spiritual growth and personal contentment, revealing the profound connection between one's financial state and inner life. This integration can bring a sense of fulfillment and spiritual enrichment to your financial journey.

1

DEBT-BANISHING SPELLS

People frequently perceive debt as simply a hindrance to economic freedom and a cause of stress. However, when viewed through a spiritual lens, the implications of debt extend far beyond the confines of one's bank account. Many traditions believe that debt holds spiritual significance, impacting personal energy and life quality.

How Debt Drains Your Energy

Within the realm of spiritual finance, debt is perceived as an energetic weight rather than a mere numerical value. It can hold individuals back from achieving their fullest potential by creating a shadow of worry and scarcity that permeates other aspects of life. This is because debt often carries with it feelings of guilt, shame, and failure, which can manifest as negative energy. This energy can stifle creativity, reduce personal vibrancy, and even affect physical health. The stress associated with managing debt can lead to anxiety and depression, which further depletes one's personal energy reserves.

How Debt Affects the Flow of Life

Debt can also disrupt the natural flow of life. In many spiritual beliefs, the flow of energy or 'chi' is crucial to maintaining balance and harmony. Debt has the potential to disrupt the flow when it becomes too burdensome. It can hinder not only financial opportunities but also personal relationships and professional growth. Constantly worrying about debt can hinder individuals from fully engaging in daily interactions and giving their best in different areas of life.

Spiritual Practices to Ease Debt's Burden

Recognizing the profound impact of debt, various spiritual practices offer methods to mitigate its negative energies. Rituals and spells in Wiccan traditions, for example, often include elements that are meant to cleanse one's financial aura. The use of herbs, candles, and crystals that correspond to prosperity, coupled with affirmations, can help clear debts and attract abundance.

Mindfulness and meditation are also powerful tools for addressing the spiritual weight of debt. By fostering a state of calm and centeredness, individuals can better navigate the stresses of debt. Practicing meditation can foster detachment from materialistic aspects of life, offering a clearer view of debt and how to manage it. This spiritual practice aids in understanding that while debt is a present reality, it does not define one's worth or capabilities.

Shifting Viewpoints on Debt

Changing your mindset from scarcity to abundance is crucial when dealing with the spiritual burden of debt. This does not mean living beyond one's means but rather cultivating a mindset that focuses on opportunities rather than limitations. In spiritual terms, this is often referred to as manifesting abundance. Through the power of belief and visualization, one can invite the energies and possibilities necessary to manifest a life free from debt.

Combining Financial and Spiritual Management

Finally, integrating financial strategies with spiritual practices offers a holistic approach to managing debt. This involves establishing practical financial objectives, developing a budget, and staying committed to them while also engaging in spiritual practices that support these goals. The synergy between pragmatic financial planning and spiritual enrichment creates a powerful framework for overcoming debt and enhancing overall well-being.

Understanding and addressing this dimension can lead to not only financial recovery but also a more fulfilled and balanced life. By combining practical strategies and spiritual insights, *Abundance Spells* shows how to gracefully navigate financial challenges and debt.

Spell for Clearing Debt

Within the realm of financial spirituality, especially in traditions like Wicca, individuals utilize spells as intentional practices to manifest specific life changes. The purpose of a clearing debt spell is to channel the practitioner's energy and intentions towards alleviating debt. This kind of spell combines symbolic materials, affirmations, and visualization to create a powerful force aimed at improving one's financial situation. Discover a detailed guide on performing a powerful spell to eliminate debt, incorporating elements that represent abundance and the release from financial burdens.

Bill Payment Booster Spell

Unlock your financial relief. Streamline your finances and meet your obligations effortlessly.

Items Needed:

- Green Candle
- Candleholder
- Patchouli Oil
- Patchouli Incense
- Pen and paper
- Cauldron

Directions:

Use the pen to draw an illustration of the bill you want to pay on the paper. Words and symbols, along with the dollar amount. Anoint the candle with the oil, and place the folded paper under the candleholder. Light the candle and the incense. Watching the flames and say:

"As the candle burns

And then lights the way

For the money that's coming

This bill will pay."

Concentrate on the particular bill and why it's essential to be paid off. Let the candle burn for about fifteen minutes, and then snuff it out. Every day, let the candle burn for another fifteen minutes, repeating the chant, for a total of seven days. On the last day, remove the paper and light it in the flame to burn completely. Let the candle keep burning at this point until it goes out naturally.

To respect the spell, any sudden money that comes your way should be used towards this bill. If you don't, you'll realize you'll just end up losing the money.

Banish Poverty Ritual

This is established in a New Orleans voodoo practice. This spell will make sure that you always have the basics in life. Reclaim prosperity and secure your financial future.

Items Needed:

- Rice
- Sugar
- Salt
- Safety Pin
- Bowl

Directions:

Fill a bowl with equal parts of rice, sugar, and salt. Open the safety pin and set it in the middle of the bowl. Keep the bowl out and visible to get rid of poverty.

Path to Debt Freedom Spell

Break free from debt and enjoy lasting security.

Items Needed:

- Myrrh Oil
- Pen
- Paper
- White Pillar Candle
- Pin

Directions:

During a new or waning moon, write a detail list of specifically what you owe, and who you owe it to. After you've created this list on the paper, carve the same list into the candle with the pin. Inscribe the candle with all of your debts, and then add a drop or two of oil onto it. Light the candle and calm your thoughts as best you can. Look into the flame of the candle, visualizing your debts evaporating away. See yourself paying off your last debts, your accounts paid and being filled with feelings of independence and simplicity. Sit with this visualization for ten minutes. Let the candle burn for ten more minutes. Repeat this each night until the candle has burned down completely. You should soon see yourself out of debt, unexpected money or a way to save money which can help pay off your debt.

Financial Rescue Spell

Navigate through tough economic times. Gain stability and peace of mind when you need it most.

Items Needed:

- Clove Oil
- Paper Money

Directions:

Trace a money symbol or rune on the largest currency bill that you have with oil while visualizing that there's always money for your needs. Put this bill in your wallet or purse, resisting the urge to spend it for as long as you can. Each time you look at the bill, visualize the symbol or rune to reinforce its power.

By combining these spiritual practices with practical financial management, you create a comprehensive approach that can significantly enhance your ability to manage and eliminate debt. These spells not only aids in focusing your intentions but also empowers you to take control of your financial destiny.

Rituals for Managing Debt-Free Living

Sustaining a life free from debt encompasses more than just clearing outstanding debts. Incorporating both pragmatic strategies and meaningful rituals can create a holistic approach to managing one's finances, making the maintenance of a debt-free life not only possible but sustainable.

Financial Control as a Ritualistic Practice

Living debt-free requires practicing financial discipline as a foundational element. This involves setting strict budgets, tracking expenses, and adhering to a financial plan that prioritizes savings and investments over unnecessary spending. By making these activities regular practices or rituals, they become integrated into a routine, making it less likely to veer off from financial goals.

- **Budgeting Ritual:** At the start of each month, perform a budgeting ritual in which you review last month's expenses, set the budget for the current month, and outline financial goals. By following this ritual, you can maintain a clear and focused mindset about your financial health.
- **Expense Tracking:** Make it a daily practice to record all expenditures. Develop a daily habit of recording all expenses, setting aside a specific time to update your financial tracker, reflecting on each expense's necessity, and adjusting future spending accordingly.

Spiritual Habits for Financial Abundance

The energy surrounding financial decisions can be amplified and a debt-free life can be maintained through the incorporation of spiritual rituals. These rituals, often rooted in various spiritual traditions, focus on setting intentions, clearing negative energies, and attracting financial stability.

- **New Moon Money Ritual:** Each new moon engages in a ritual to set financial intentions for the cycle ahead. Jot down your financial goals, light a green candle for prosperity, and meditate on your intentions.
- **Regular Cleansing of Spaces:** Physical spaces can accumulate negative energy that might affect financial decision-making. Regularly sage your home or workspace to prevent impulsive spending or financial neglect caused by negative energies.

Emotional Strategies to Reinforce Debt-Free Living

The psychological aspect of maintaining a debt-free lifestyle is crucial. It involves understanding the emotional triggers that lead to unnecessary spending and using strategies to counteract them.

- **Mindfulness Practices:** Incorporate mindfulness into your financial habits by being fully present during each purchase decision. Before making a non-essential purchase, take a moment to assess whether this aligns with your long-term financial goals.
- **Gratitude Journaling:** Keep a daily gratitude journal focused on what you already have. This practice can shift your mindset from one of lack (which can lead to spending as an attempt to fill a void) to one of abundance, reducing the urge to gain new debts.

Community Engagement and Accountability

Creating a community or finding a group that shares the goal of debt-free living can provide support and accountability. Regular meetings or check-ins can serve as a ritual that reinforces commitment to this lifestyle.

- **Debt-Free Community Rituals:** take part in or start a debt-free club where members share tips, successes, and challenges. These meetings can include rituals such as sharing a financial victory or setting a group financial challenge for the month.

Continuous Education and Transformation

Consistently staying debt-free involves ongoing learning and adapting to new financial knowledge and resources. Regularly set aside time to learn about personal finance and investment strategies, whether through books, courses, or workshops.

- **Educational Rituals:** Dedicate the first weekend of every quarter to reviewing new financial tools, reading an economic book, or attending a workshop. By doing this, you can stay informed and be proactive in managing your finances.

By integrating these practices into your lifestyle, you establish a robust framework for living without debt. These practical and spiritual rituals strengthen the discipline, mindfulness, and intention required for long-term financial freedom.

2

ALIGNING CAREER WITH SPIRITUAL PURPOSE

Aligning your career with your spiritual purpose is a transformative journey that can bring about profound changes in your life. It's not just about finding a job that pays the bills but about discovering a profession that resonates with your soul. This alignment can lead to increased job satisfaction, improved mental health, and a sense of contributing to something greater than yourself. By aligning your career with your spiritual purpose, you can create a life that is not just financially rewarding but also deeply fulfilling.

Understanding Spiritual Purpose

The journey to aligning your career with your spiritual purpose begins with understanding what 'spiritual purpose' means to you. It involves reflecting on your deepest values, your passions, and your innate skills. Ask yourself what brings you joy, what activities give you a sense of peace, and what naturally draws you. These reflections are not just about identifying what you enjoy, but also discerning what makes you feel fulfilled and deeply connected to something larger than yourself.

Self-Assessment and Reflection

A crucial step in this alignment is thorough self-assessment. Tools like personality tests, strength finders, or even meditation and journaling can help uncover your true self. During this exploration, you should focus on identifying your key strengths and how you can apply them in a professional context. Considering experiences that brought significant satisfaction or spiritual fulfillment can provide insights into what environments or industries are best suited for you.

Careers That Foster Spiritual Growth

Specific careers naturally lend themselves to a greater sense of purpose and fulfillment. For instance, roles in nonprofits, social enterprises, education, healthcare, and creative fields often align with individuals seeking to make a direct and meaningful impact on the world. However, any career can become spiritually fulfilling if it matches your personal values and allows you to engage in work that feels meaningful and contributes to a more significant cause.

Integrating Spirituality and Professional Growth

Once you have a clear idea of what feels spiritually fulfilling, the next step is to integrate this understanding into your career planning. This might mean pivoting to a new field that resonates more with your spiritual goals or incorporating your values into your current job. It could also involve advocating for roles or projects within your workplace that align more closely with your values.

For those transitioning to an alternative career path, practical steps such as additional training, networking in the desired field, or starting as a volunteer can facilitate this shift. For others, minor changes, such as starting a workplace wellness program or leading a community service project, can infuse a current role with greater purpose.

Overcoming Challenges

Aligning your career with your spiritual purpose is challenging. You must also address financial considerations, job market realities, and personal obligations when aligning your career with your spiritual purpose. It's essential to plan strategically, setting realistic goals and timelines for your career transition. Consulting with career coaches or mentors who understand your spiritual goals can provide guidance and support.

Continuous Re-evaluation

Remember, aligning your career with your spiritual purpose is not a one-time task, but a continuous process of self-discovery and growth. As you grow, your spiritual needs may change, and it's essential to ensure that your career continues to meet these needs. Regular self-reflection and reassessment of your career path can help you stay on track and maintain a fulfilling, integrated life.

Aligning your career with your spiritual purpose is about creating a life where your professional endeavors extend your deepest self. It involves understanding your values, leveraging your strengths, and making deliberate choices to ensure that your work not only supports you financially but also contributes to your overall life's purpose. This alignment is crucial not just for career satisfaction but for a fulfilling, integrated life.

Spells for Career Advancement

Career advancement is not solely a matter of experience and education; many also believe that a spiritual boost can significantly influence one's professional trajectory. For those inclined towards incorporating mystical practices into their career strategy, spells and rituals for career advancement can serve as powerful tools. These rituals aim to enhance personal energy, attract professional opportunities, and clear obstacles in the path to success.

Understanding the Role of Spells in Career Advancement

Spells for career advancement are based on the principle that positive intentions and directed energy can influence tangible outcomes. These spells often use symbols of success, communication, and influence, aligning your spiritual path with your career goals. This method intends not only to bring about specific changes but also to shift the surrounding energy, making you a magnet for opportunities and professional growth.

Essential Elements of Career Advancement Spells

Effective spells for enhancing career growth often include several key elements:

- **Yellow Candles:** Yellow represents intellect, creativity, and persuasion, qualities essential for career success. Lighting a yellow candle can be seen as igniting one's intelligence and charisma.
- **Herbs like Rosemary and Mint:** Rosemary is associated with mental clarity and loyalty and is helpful in job performance and office politics, while mint stimulates communication and innovation.
- **Tiger's Eye Crystal:** Known for its grounding and protection properties, Tiger's Eye can also bring luck and clarity, helping to make strategic career decisions.
- **Feathers:** Feathers symbolize communication and inspirational thinking, and individuals can use them in spells to enhance these aspects of work life.

A Simple Ritual for Career Advancement

1. **Preparation:** Choose a time when you are undisturbed and focused, ideally during a waxing moon, symbolizing growth. Cleanse your space by burning sage or incense to remove negative energy and create a conducive environment.

2. **Set Your Altar:** Place a yellow candle in the center of your altar. Arrange rosemary and mint around it, and position the Tiger's Eye crystal prominently near the candle base. If available, include a feather from any bird known for its keen sight or flight, such as an eagle or hawk.

3. **Casting the Spell:**

- Light the yellow candle, focusing on the flame as a symbol of the energy you wish to bring to your career.
- Hold the Tiger's Eye in your dominant hand and visualize your career aspirations as clearly as possible. See yourself achieving your next career milestone, feeling the satisfaction and recognition that comes with it.
- Sprinkle some rosemary and mint leaves over the flame (carefully, ensuring not to start a fire), and say, "Clarity and creativity guide my way, bring about my career success day by day."
- Wave the feather gently in the air above the candle flame, symbolizing the transmission of your intentions to the universe and enhancing your communicative powers within your career space.

4. **Closing the Ritual:** If possible, allow the candle to burn down completely under supervision, solidifying your intentions into the universe. Carry the Tiger's Eye with you to important meetings or interviews as a talisman.

5. **Regular Reinforcement:** Repeat this ritual quarterly or during significant career transitions, such as before a performance review, when applying for a promotion, or when embarking on substantial projects.

Integrating Practical Actions

A well-rounded approach to career advancement involves combining spiritual practices with practical efforts like networking and continuous professional development. This combination of the spiritual and the practical creates a balanced strategy, making career growth not only possible but also more likely.

Career advancement spells encompass more than mere desires for success.

Spells and Rituals for Professional Success

Career advancement spells and rituals harness the spiritual realm to boost personal energy, attract opportunities, and remove obstacles for professional growth.

Career Catalyst Salt Spell

Accelerate your career path. Enhance your job prospects and secure your dream position.

Items Needed:

- Salt

Directions:

Before going to an interview, carry three grains of salt with you. When at the place of employment, throw the salt towards the north corner of the interview area. It is said that in three days, you will have the position.

Job Acquisition Candle Ritual

Light the way to your next job with. Spark opportunities and attract the ideal employment.

Items Needed:

- Green Candle
- Red Candle
- Straight Pin

Directions:

This spell should be applied after you have given your resume or application. With the pin, write the name of the firm you choose to work for on the front of the green candle. On the red candle, you will etch the victory rune Tiwaz, (↑) with your complete name. Burn both candles for thirty minutes on a Thursday after the sun sets. Visualizing yourself having the type of work you prefer. At the conclusion of the thirty minutes, snuff the candles. Burn them each Thursday after that for fifteen minutes until they burn out, or until you receive the position. Dispose of the candles and leave behind a small bowl of milk outside overnight as a gift.

Employment Attraction Incense Ritual

Surround yourself with the aroma of opportunity. Boost job search success effortlessly.

Items Needed:

- 1 tbsp. Frankincense
- 1 tbsp. Basil
- 2 tsp. Sandalwood

- 2 tsp. Wormwood
- 2 tsp. Vervain
- 1 tsp. Cedar Wood
- 1 tsp. Mace
- 1 tsp. Cinnamon
- 1 Charcoal Disc

Directions:

Mix herbs and empower. Burn mixture on charcoal disc when seeking employment.

Ultimate Success Spell

Achieve unparalleled success. Propel yourself to the top with powerful, proven magical support.

Items Needed:

- White Sign (Poster) Board You Can Sit On
- Blue Pen

Directions:

On a Monday 7 p.m., begin by having a bath or shower. Once you've dried yourself thoroughly, stay undressed and move into an area where you will be uninterrupted. Put the signboard on the floor and outline on it a wide circle in a clockwise direction using the blue pen. Stand within the circle, lifting your arms upwards taking a few deep breaths. Once completed, set yourself in the middle of the circle and say:

"By the influence of these numbers,

By the strength of Fortuna,

All that rests within this circle shall blossom."

Write the following numbers 7, 11, 9 on the signboard, with the number making a triangle saying:

"Now my circle is cast,

And the magick here will last.

And as my will, so mote it be."

Keep the signboard in a secure place and sit on it each time you have to carry out a decision on a matter.

Job Attraction Spell

Secure your ideal job. Designed to draw career opportunities directly to you.

Items Needed:

- Your Favorite Color Candle
- 2 Brown Candles
- Green Candle
- Prosperity Incense
- Prosperity Oil
- Charcoal Disc

Directions:

Burn prosperity incense. On the evening of the New Moon, Anoint the candles with prosperity oil. Anointing from wick to end. In the center, place the brown candle. On the right, the green candle and your color candle on the left. Light your color candle and declare:

"I want for change, this is my right,

I clear the road, and free my sight."

Ignite the green and state:

"Good luck is mine as is the success,

Support me Great Ones, and draw closer to me."

Light the brown and say:

"Prospects, work, and rewards I see,

And as my will, so mote it be."

Allow candles to burn out entirely and dispose of the wax afterward. Light the second brown candle while meditating, visualizing for nine minutes and gaining balance in preparing for the position and the satisfaction to come from it. Burn each night until the candle is consumed up. During this time period, aggressively search for a job. Listen to your instinct and stay on all leads.

Wealth-Boosting Prosperity Incense

Ignite your financial growth. Crafted to enhance wealth and attract abundance.

Items Needed:

- 1 Part Frankincense
- 1 Part Cinnamon
- 1 Part Dried Lemon Peel
- 1 Part Dried Orange Peel
- 1 Part Nutmeg
- 2 Drops Frankincense Oil
- 1 Drop Cinnamon Oil

Directions:

Mix dry ingredients together as you visualize on the incense's goal. Add in the oil. Once thoroughly mixed, empower the incense again. Burn on a charcoal disc. Place the unused portion in a jar with lid and store in dark cool place.

Abundance Amplifying Prosperity Oil

Apply increase in wealth flow. Perfect for magnifying financial gains.

Items Needed:

- 3 Drops Frankincense Oil
- 2 Drops Cinnamon Oil
- 1 Drop Nutmeg Oil
- 1 Drop Cinnamon Oil
- Base Oil of Your Choice
- Glass Jar

Directions:

Add your essential oil to a ¼ cup of a base oil such as Coconut, Jojoba, Grape Seed, in a clean glass jar. Add the essential a drop at a time gently mixing. Store oils away from heat, light, humidity. Remember to identify your jar.

Job Acquisition Magic

Transform your career prospects. Harness potent energies to land the perfect job swiftly.

Items Needed:

- Green Candle
- Dollar Bill
- Picture of Yourself
- Paper Clip

Directions:

Before going to your job interview, light a green candle then displayed both sides of a dollar bill to the candle's flame. Fold the bill into thirds, slipping your picture inside and fasten together with the paper clip. Carry you dollar/picture packet in your purse, pocketbook or wallet.

Salary Boosting Spell

Elevate your earnings with a Salary Boosting Spell. Crafted to enhance your persuasive power and secure the raise you deserve.

Items Needed:

- Green Candle
- Pine Oil
- Pen
- Dollar Bill
- Green Cloth
- Recent Pay Stub (a photocopy will do)

Directions:

Gather at the objects together on the first evening of the full moon. Inscribe your employer's name on the candle. Under his name, carve an arrow pointing down the candle, accompanied by a dollar sign and then another candle pointing down. While visualizing your desire for a raise, anoint the candle. On your pay stub, print the sum of the raise you require under your net amount. Add the two figures together and circle. Place your pay stub under the candle. Light the candle as you envision your boss granting a raise for you. Say:

"From you to me the money will flow.

Casting out my financial woes

The raise I desire shall be approved

In advance of the light

Of the following Full Moon."

Let the candle burn down thoroughly. Wrap the remnants of the candle in green cloth and bring with you. Ask your boss for the raise on a Wednesday before the next Full Moon.

Creating a Magical Workspace

The key to a magical workspace is more than just how it looks. By combining tangible adjustments and intangible practices, this process turns your work area into an inspiring and efficient sanctuary.

Physical Arrangement and Organization

A magical workspace's physical arrangement forms its foundation. A clean, organized desk free from clutter is essential, as clutter can hinder concentration and block the flow of creative energy. Begin by organizing your workspace, making sure everything is in its designated spot. Utilizing organizational tools such as drawer dividers, cable organizers, and document holders can help maintain an orderly environment that is conducive to focus and clarity.

Natural Elements

Including nature-inspired elements can greatly enhance the liveliness of a workspace. Plants are particularly effective as they not only beautify the space but also improve air quality and bring in life force energy. Opt for plants with air-purifying qualities, like peace lilies or spider plants. Additionally, natural light is a potent enhancer of energy; whenever possible, arrange your workspace so that it receives plenty of sunlight. If you don't have enough natural light, think about using full-spectrum light bulbs that replicate natural light.

Color Psychology

Colors have a profound impact on our mood and energy levels. The correct color choice for your workspace can enhance productivity and creativity. Blue stimulates the mind, promoting concentration and calmness; green creates a sense of balance and relaxation; yellow inspires creativity; and red energizes. Pick colors that best resonate with your work goals, taking into consideration your profession and personal energy needs.

Personal Touches and Symbolic Items

Adding meaningful items to your workspace can greatly enhance its magical qualities. These might include photographs of loved ones, inspirational quotes, or artwork that uplifts and motivates you. Also, think about including symbols or objects that align with your spiritual beliefs, like crystals, tarot cards, or statues of deities or spiritual figures. For instance, amethyst is believed to promote clarity of thought, while citrine is said to attract wealth and success.

Aromatherapy and Sound

Scents and sounds can powerfully influence the atmosphere of a workspace. An oil diffuser can be used to create a calming, focused, or energizing environment with essential oils like lavender, lemon, and rosemary. Choose scents based on your needs; for example, peppermint can invigorate the senses and enhance concentration, while lavender can help reduce stress. Similarly, background sounds or music can set the tone for your workday. Nature sounds, classical music, and even specific frequencies like binaural beats can promote a calm and productive mindset.

Rituals and Intentions

Start your workday with a brief ritual to set intentions and cleanse the energy. It could include lighting a candle, setting a daily objective, or taking a few minutes to meditate or pray. Engaging in such practices allows you to establish a deeper connection with your work and maintain a focused energy throughout the day.

Ergonomics and Comfort

Your workspace must be physically comfortable, without a doubt. Invest in an ergonomic chair that supports your back, use a keyboard and mouse that minimize strain on your wrists, and set your monitor at eye level to avoid neck pain. Being physically comfortable not only reduces the risk of injury but also improves focus and productivity.

When these elements are integrated, your workspace becomes more dynamic and supportive. It transforms into a space that fosters both creativity and well-being, enabling optimal performance and enjoyment while working.

3

THE NATURE OF LUCK AND HOW TO INFLUENCE IT

Finance often gives the impression that luck is a capricious and elusive force that gives blessings on a few and overlooks the rest. However, the concept of luck is more complex and fluid, and understanding its nature can significantly influence personal and business financial success. Individuals can position themselves to take advantage of seemingly coincidental opportunities by examining the psychological, strategic, and spiritual dimensions of luck.

Psychological Aspects of Luck

When studying luck, psychologists have frequently discovered that one's mindset is vital for recognizing and capitalizing on lucky chances. Dr. Richard Wiseman, in his extensive research, identified that individuals who consider themselves lucky are often more open to possibilities, more optimistic, and have a broader network of relationships. These characteristics allow them to identify and capitalize on overlooked opportunities.

To cultivate a lucky mindset:

- **Expect good fortune:** Simply believing in good luck can increase confidence, which motivates more decisive action and openness to opportunities.
- **Stay open to new experiences:** Embracing the unknown and stepping out of comfort zones increases the likelihood of encountering beneficial situations.
- **Maintain a positive outlook:** Optimism enables individuals to persist in the face of setbacks, increasing the chances of eventually experiencing positive outcomes.

Strategic Approach to Luck

Through informed decisions and planning, individuals can strategically shape their luck in financial matters. This involves understanding market trends, making educated investments, and strategically positioning oneself in situations where opportunities are likely to arise. Take an investor who diversifies their portfolio across emerging markets. They may 'luckily' come across a high-growth startup, but only because they positioned themselves in a place where such opportunities are more common.

To enhance financial luck through strategy:

- **Diversify investments:** Spreading resources across different sectors and investments minimizes risks and increases the chance of hitting upon a lucrative opportunity.
- **Network actively:** Building and maintaining a broad network can lead to inside information or helpful business opportunities.
- **Stay informed:** Keeping abreast of financial news and trends can alert you to emerging opportunities before they become mainstream.

Spiritual and Esoteric Perspectives on Luck

Various cultures and spiritual traditions incorporate rituals to attract good fortune, especially in finance. These range from Feng Shui arrangements that attract wealth to spells and charms in pagan traditions to prayers and blessings in various religious practices. Although skeptics question the direct effects of these rituals, believers often experience heightened confidence and peace of mind, which can indirectly shape financial choices.

To attract luck through spiritual means:

- **Use symbols of wealth and prosperity:** In Feng Shui, placing objects like the laughing Buddha or golden toads near the business area can attract wealth.
- **Practice gratitude and generosity:** Many spiritual traditions believe that what you give returns to you manifold. Regular charity and expressions of gratitude can create a positive cycle of prosperity.
- **Regularly clear your space of negative energy:** Whether through smudging with sage, using crystals, or prayer, keeping your environment energetically clean can promote a positive and 'lucky' atmosphere.

Realistic Perspective on Luck

Financial success is ultimately a combination of luck, hard work, and wise planning. Those who are 'lucky' in finance often work diligently and make intelligent decisions that increase their odds of encountering favorable outcomes. By adopting a more comprehensive approach to effectively managing finances, individuals can see luck as something influenced by attitude, strategy, and spiritual practices.

Spells to Enhance Financial Luck

In the quest for financial prosperity, the concept of "luck" often plays a fascinating role. While some may attribute luck to mere chance or coincidence, within the realm of magical practice, it is an energy that intentional action can influence. These spells, rooted in various traditions, aim to align your energy with the forces of abundance and prosperity, helping you to attract financial opportunities.

Understanding the Basis of Luck Spells

Financial luck spells are not about conjuring money out of thin air; instead, they work on the principle of enhancing the flow of prosperity towards you. They involve clearing energy blockages, setting focused intentions, and using specific items that resonate with wealth attraction. The effectiveness of these spells often hinges on the practitioner's belief and the energy put into the ritual.

Key Elements of Financial Luck Spells

When performing spells for financial luck, people use certain common elements known for their metaphysical properties associated with wealth. These include:

- **Green Candles:** Green is the color of money and is often used to attract prosperity. Lighting a green candle during a spell supposedly draws wealth towards you.
- **Citrine:** This crystal is known for its properties of wealth attraction and maintaining wealth. Holding a piece of citrine while visualizing financial success can enhance the spell's effectiveness.
- **Basil:** Known as the "money magnet" among herbs, basil is used in spells either by sprinkling it around

candles or carrying it in a pouch to attract financial luck.

- **Gold Coins:** Symbols of wealth. Gold coins are used in spells either physically or symbolically, to represent the wealth being attracted.

Step-by-Step Financial Luck Spell

1. **Setting Up Your Space:** Choose a quiet time and place where you won't be disturbed. Cleanse your space by burning sage or incense to remove negative energies and create a conducive environment for your spell.

2. **Prepare Your Materials:** Gather your green candle, a piece of citrine, a few basil leaves, and a gold coin. Arrange them on a small table or altar where you will perform your spell.

3. **Casting the Spell:**

- Light the green candle and focus on the flame. Visualize it, burning away financial obstacles.
- Hold the citrine in your dominant hand and visualize your financial goals as already achieved. Feel the joy and security that comes with financial success.
- Place the basil leaves around the candle base and the gold coin in front of the candle. As you do this, say out loud or in your mind: "Wealth flows, wealth grows, obstacles go, prosperity shows."
- Allow the candle to burn down safely and carry the citrine and basil with you in the days following the spell to continue attracting financial luck.

4. **Closing the Spell:** Thank the elements and energies that assisted in your ritual. Dispose of the candle remnants respect-

fully and keep the citrine and gold coin in your wallet or purse to keep drawing wealth.

Maintaining the Luck

Spells for financial luck are most effective when combined with practical efforts. Continue to manage your finances wisely, look for opportunities, and be open to unexpected sources of income. Regularly revisiting your spell and renewing it can also help maintain its effectiveness, aligning your spirit continuously with the energy of prosperity.

By integrating these magical practices into your life, you can enhance your financial luck and open doors to new possibilities. Remember, the real magic often lies in your actions and intentions, supported by the ritualistic work of the spells.

Fortune's Favor Numbers Spell

Amplify your luck. Designed to boost your chances in games of chance and daily luck.

Items Needed:

- Pendulum
- 1 Green Candle
- Sprigs of Sweet Grass, Lemon Balm, and Borage
- Pine Incense
- Paper
- Green Marker

Directions:

A pendulum can be a straightforward item that is suspended from a string, so if you don't have a "true" pendulum, you can create your own for this spell. With the green marker, draw a septagram (shown below) on the paper and stack the herbs up in the middle of the star.

Nearby, light the candle and incense.

Holding the pendulum at the end of its string allowing the bob or object dangles in the middle of the circle. At this time, you must now think about picking that winning number.

First, concentrate on the first number in the series. Start by asserting "1" out loud and observing the pendulum. If it achieves nothing, state "2" and so forth. At some stage, it will produce a wobble and you should jot that as your first number. Continue to the following digit to the point you have written all the numbers you require for your specific lottery.

Instant Win Scratch-Off Spell

Unlock a world of wins. Increase your odds for scratch-off lottery success dramatically."

Items Needed:

- 5 Dry Corn Kernels
- 3 Acorns

- Malachite Gemstone

Directions:

Hold the corn kernels and acorns between your hands in addition to the malachite gemstone. Rub your hands together, maintaining the seeds and nuts in your hands. Repeat the following:

"With these nuts and seeds,

Is where wealth leads.

To mix and match,

I choose a scratch."

Continue to rub your hands together, while all the pieces drop out from your hands. The day following you do this spell, insert the malachite gemstone in your hand while you are picking out a scratch ticket you want.

Ultimate Luck Mojo Bag

Carry the power of luck everywhere. Ideal for enhancing fortune in all aspects of life.

Items Needed:

- 1 Green Bag
- Green Cord
- 1 tbsp. Basil
- 1 tbsp. Irish Moss
- 1 tbsp. Lilacs
- 1 tbsp. Clove

Directions:

Add each herb into the green bag closing it securely with the cord. Consecrate and charge the bag. Keep the charm bag with you at all as it will bring in good luck.

Prosperity's Charm Bag

Elevate your luck. Perfect for attracting wealth and positive energy wherever you go

Items Needed:

- Apache Tear
- 7 Star Anise Seeds
- 7 Inch Gold Ribbon
- 5 Inch Square Yellow or Gold Fabric

Directions:

Put the Apache tear in the middle of the fabric. Add the star anise one at a time while reciting:

"One is for luck,

Two is for money.

Three is the favor,

Four for honey.

Five is for old,

Six is for new.

Seven will bring to me success,

In all that I do."

Pull up the edges of the material and secure the sachet with the gold ribbon. Carry the charm with you every day.

Enchanted Luck Witch Candle Ritual

Ignite your fortune. Specifically crafted to enhance your luck and attract prosperity.

Items Needed:

- Orange Candle
- Cinnamon Oil

Directions:

At midnight, anoint the candle with oil. Light the candle and repeat three times:

"Brimstone, moon, and witch's fire,

Candlelight shining spell.

Good luck will I now acquire,

Work your magic well.

Midnight is the witching hour,

Bring me the luck that I seek.

By three times three, I feel your power,

As these words, now I speak.

Harming none, my spell is done.

As my will, so mote it be."

Wish Fulfillment Spell

Make your deepest desires come true. Tailored to manifest your wishes into reality.

Items Needed:

- Green candle

- Green or white paper

Directions:

On the evening of the New Moon, print your request on a plain piece of paper. Light your white candle and turn off the lights. Focus on the success of your wish for several minutes. Continue to think about your wish while you burn the paper in the candle. Repeat the same time until the Full Moon.

Note: This is a wish spell and essentially I have it adapted for money, but you can apply it for just about anything using the correct corresponding color for your candle.

Maintaining a Lucky Mindset

Developing daily habits is crucial for nurturing a lucky mindset as they prepare your mental and emotional states to identify and take advantage of fortunate opportunities. This mindset isn't just about wishing for the best possible scenario; Here are strategies and daily practices that can help sustain a lucky streak in both personal and professional life.

Visualization and Affirmations

One powerful technique for sustaining a lucky mindset is the practice of visualization. This involves regularly imagining achieving your goals in vivid detail. When you visualize success, such as closing a big deal or receiving a promotion, you align your subconscious mind with your goals, increasing your awareness of potential opportunities.

When combined with visualization, daily affirmations can strengthen a mindset that attracts good luck. Starting the day by affirming positive outcomes—such as "I am open to new opportunities" or "Today, I attract luck and prosperity"—sets a positive tone and focuses your mind on what you wish to attract.

Gratitude Journaling

Gratitude is a powerful tool for maintaining a lucky mindset. When you concentrate on what you already possess and show gratitude for it, you change your perspective from what is missing to what is plentiful. This shift in perspective can significantly affect how you interact with the world, making you more receptive to new opportunities and more likely to generate the 'luck' you seek. Keeping a daily journal of things you appreciate can help you stay in a mindset of abundance and attract what you desire.

Networking and Social Interactions

Luck often comes from outside—through the people we meet and the relationships we cultivate. By actively maintaining your social and professional network, you increase your chances of coming across unique opportunities that may not be accessible through individual efforts. Engaging with various social groups, attending industry meetups, or even taking part in community activities can enhance your chances of a lucky break.

Practicing kindness and generosity in your interactions also helps sustain a lucky streak. These behaviors endear you to others, leading to a reciprocation of goodwill that manifests in fortunate opportunities.

Regular Learning and Curiosity

Keeping a curious mindset and a lifelong learning attitude can also contribute to being 'lucky.' This can be as simple as reading widely, taking courses related to your field, or exploring new hobbies that challenge your thinking and expand your horizons.

Mindfulness and Meditation

The practice of mindfulness and meditation affects mental health and the ability to maintain a positive mindset. By engaging in regular meditation, one can eliminate negativity and stress, resulting in improved clarity of thought and the ability to make positive decisions. Mindfulness helps in being present and aware, which ensures you do not miss subtle cues or opportunities that could lead to what one might call 'luck.'

Adaptability and Openness to Change

To maintain a lucky mindset, one must be adaptable and open to change. The willingness to step outside your comfort zone and embrace new challenges can lead to unexpected adventures and lucky breaks. Embracing flexibility and openness to new ideas positions you to seize opportunities that others may avoid, continuing your streak of luck.

Transforming luck from sporadic chance to a regular phenomenon in your life requires commitment and consistency in implementing these practices. By cultivating a fortunate mindset, you not only boost the likelihood of coming across positive opportunities but also improve your ability to seize them when they appear.

4

WEALTH MAGNETISM

Within Wicca, a modern religion of paganism and witchcraft, the idea of wealth encompasses more than just gathering material riches. It incorporates a broad and spiritually enriched understanding of what it means to be truly wealthy. Wealth, from a Wiccan perspective, encompasses personal well-being, community health, and ecological balance, not just financial success.

The Spiritual Dimension of Wealth

Wicca's view on wealth is strongly influenced by its emphasis on the interconnectedness of all things. Practitioners of Wicca often see wealth as a flow of energy and a reflection of the health of this interconnected web. Wiccans view true wealth as a harmonious and fulfilling life that acknowledges interconnectedness. This idea promotes the pursuit of prosperity without harming others or the environment, while prioritizing the welfare of the community and the natural world.

Wealth and the Wiccan Rede

The Wiccan Rede, "An it harm none, do what ye will," is a fundamental ethical guideline in Wicca that also applies to how Wiccans view wealth. This principle advises against pursuing wealth if it negatively impacts others or the environment. Therefore, Wiccans encourage themselves to earn and use money in ways that reflect their values and ethics. Their support is for practices and companies that advance sustainability, equity, and the betterment of society.

The Role of Magic in Attracting Wealth

In Wicca, rituals and spells are commonly used to attract and manifest wealth. These magical practices often involve setting intentions clearly, using symbols of wealth like coins, green candles (representing money), or herbs like basil and cinnamon that are believed to attract financial success. Nonetheless, these spells go beyond mere appeals for financial prosperity from the universe. This might mean working diligently towards one's goals or being wise in financial management, reinforcing the idea that magic works in tandem with practical efforts.

The Importance of Giving Back

Generosity is another significant aspect of the Wiccan view of wealth. Maintaining the flow of prosperity requires giving back, be it through charity, community service, or supporting friends and family. This practice is based on the belief that wealth should circulate and that by giving to others, one opens up space to receive more in return. Creating a balance between giving and receiving is key to maintaining the community's health and prosperity.

Balance and Moderation

The Wiccan belief system values balance and moderation when it comes to wealth. The Wiccan philosophy on wealth emphasizes caution towards excess, as it can lead to imbalances in one's life and the broader community. Wiccans advocate for living within one's means and focusing on non-material forms of wealth, such as spiritual growth, relationships, and personal happiness. Wiccans consider wealth as a tool to foster a meaningful and morally upright lifestyle, rather than an ultimate goal.

Connection with Nature

From a Wiccan perspective, wealth is often understood in terms of their bond with nature. This includes recognizing and appreciating the abundance that the Earth provides and understanding that true wealth comes from living in harmony with the natural world. Engaging in gardening, foraging, and herbalism not only physically connects us with nature, but also acknowledges the Earth as a source of both material and spiritual abundance.

Through these perspectives, the Wiccan philosophy of wealth presents a different understanding of prosperity. It encourages a broader, more spiritually and ethically informed approach. It encourages people to redefine wealth to promote personal fulfillment, community well-being, and ecological harmony, emphasizing that true prosperity encompasses more than just money.

Wealth Attraction Spells

Ancient belief connects wealth attraction spells to the concept of directing energies for manifesting desires, such as financial abundance. These rituals and spells serve as powerful tools to focus intent and invoke the energies of abundance and wealth. By harmonizing spiritual vibrations with the frequency of prosperity, individuals can attract financial opportunities, manifesting their wealth goals.

Understanding Wealth Attraction Spells

Wealth attraction spells work based on the belief that the universe is an endless source of abundance for those who know how to access it. These spells do not create wealth out of thin air; rather, they enhance the practitioner's ability to attract and recognize opportunities for wealth creation. The success of these spells relies on clear intention, strong belief, and the power to visualize and make things happen.

Critical Elements of Wealth Attraction Spells

Practitioners commonly use certain elements in wealth attraction spells for their symbolic associations and reputed metaphysical properties.

- **Green Candles:** Green is the color of money, growth, and prosperity. Lighting green candles during wealth spells is intended to draw financial growth.
- **Citrine and Pyrite:** These crystals are popular in money spells. Citrine attracts wealth and abundance, while pyrite is associated with wealth and good luck.
- **Patchouli and Basil:** Herbs play significant roles in spells; patchouli is associated with abundance, while basil draws in wealth and luck.
- **Gold Coins or Paper Money:** Using these items can symbolically attract more money into one's life.

A Simple Wealth Attraction Spell

1. **Preparation:** Find a quiet space where you can focus without interruptions, ideally during the waxing moon phase, which symbolizes growth and increase. Cleanse the area with sage or incense to remove negative energies, setting a pure stage for your intentions.

2. **Set Your Altar:** Arrange your green candle at the center of your altar. Surround it with citrine and pyrite crystals. Place patchouli leaves and basil around these, and have a few gold coins or a small amount of paper money in front of the candle.

3. **Casting the Spell:**

- Light the green candle, focusing on the flame and visualizing it growing into financial abundance.
- Hold the citrine crystal in your hands, closing your eyes, and vividly imagine achieving your financial goals, such as paying off debt, saving for a big purchase, or achieving financial freedom.
- Sprinkle basil and patchouli around the base of the candle as you chant, "Abundance flow, prosperity grow, wealth come, it will be done."
- Place the gold coins or money near the candle's flame carefully (ensuring they do not catch fire) as a symbolic act of attracting more money.

4. **Closing the Spell:** Let the candle burn down entirely if possible, always under supervision for safety. This symbolizes the complete transmission of your desires from the spiritual to the material realm. Carry the citrine with you in your wallet or purse to continue attracting wealth.

5. **Maintaining the Energy:** To keep the spell's energy active, repeat the ritual regularly each month during the waxing moon

and reinforce your intention with positive affirmations about wealth and abundance.

Integrating Practical Financial Actions

When casting wealth attraction spells, it's important to combine spiritual practices with practical financial habits. This includes budgeting effectively, seeking investment opportunities, and continuously educating yourself on financial matters. Aligning spiritual actions with practical steps enhances your potential to attract and retain wealth.

Through these rituals, wealth attraction spells promote long-lasting financial growth by combining spiritual depth and practical wisdom, aiming to transform both your finances and your mindset towards money.

Abundance Enhancing Prosperity Powder

Sprinkle your path to wealth. Ideal for boosting financial gains and success.

Items Needed:

- 2 parts Cinnamon
- 1 parts Myrrh
- 1 parts Allspice
- 1 parts Cloves
- 1/2 part Basil
- 1/2 part Patchouli

Directions:

Pulverize in a mortar and pestle. Dust in your purse, pocketbook, wallet, over your checkbooks or ledgers. Store the unused quantity in a jar with a lid and keep in a dark cool place.

Cinnamon Wealth Attraction Spell

Harness the power of cinnamon to attract wealth. This Cinnamon Wealth Attraction Spell brings financial abundance directly to you.

Items Needed:

- Cinnamon
- Green Candle
- Six Coins
- Green Pouch

Directions:

Form a circle, using the coins, around the candle. Once the candle is lit, repeat three times:

"As cash flows,

As wealth grows,

The money will shine,

Money is mine."

Sprinkle the pouch with cinnamon. While gathering the coins and depositing them in the pouch say:

"Draw money to me,

Three times three"

Carry the pouch on you.

Financial Fortune Mojo Bag

Carry the power of wealth. A potent charm for drawing money and enhancing economic opportunities.

Items Needed:

- Ginger
- Nutmeg
- Silver Candle
- Gold Candle
- Small Cloth Pouch with a Drawstring
- Play Money
- Magickal Tag Lock Of Yourself (Nail Clippings, Hair, Photo, etc.)

Directions:

Light the two silver candles on whichever position of your altar or space since you are working between them. As you light them, declare:

"Gold and silver, silver and gold,

Make money arrive and dollars unfold."

Place play money and the magickal tag lock of yourself into the pouch. While performing this, see yourself and the money. Say:

"I cast this from necessity, and not from greed,

All I'm calling for is what I need."

Put the ginger and the nutmeg in the pouch. Envision success and prosperity moving your way. Take the pouch in your hands and declare:

"Ones and fives, tens and twenties

As my will, so mote it be!"

Take a minute to realize what you will accomplish with the money as it moves your way. Allow the candles to burn out by themselves. Set the pouch in a secure place where it will be undisturbed, and place out of sight.

Luxurious Wealth Attraction Bath

Soak in success. Crafted to cleanse away financial obstacles and draw prosperity.

Items Needed:

- Sea Salt
- 3 drops Basil Oil
- 3 drops Cinnamon Oil
- 3 drops Pine Oil
- Dash of Patchouli Herb
- A Small Bottle with a Tight Cap

Directions:

Run a pleasant bath and adding the salt, oils, and herbs to the water. Have a nice soak for at least fifteen minutes. While in the tub, visualize the coming event that will draw you money and what you call for the result to be.

Before emptying the water, fill the bottle with the bathwater, securely closing it. Carry it with you to the meeting.

Abundance Welcome Home Spell

Invite prosperity into your living space. Perfect for manifesting wealth at your doorstep.

Items Needed:

- Sandalwood Chips
- Basil Leaves
- Patchouli

- Front Door Mat
- Silver Coin

Directions:

Raising up your doormat, dust the sandalwood, basil and patchouli under it. Put the coin in the middle. Stand on the mat, facing north and recite:

"I welcome abundance into my home.

It ends here, it does not stray.

My welcome mat is here for me,

Drawing in prosperity."

Sevenfold Prosperity Candle Spell

Light the way to financial success. Designed to multiply your monetary gains quickly.

Items Needed:

- 7 Green Candles
- 7 Coins

Directions:

During the New Moon, set the seven coins in a circle, and with the seven candles on top. Say:

"Essence of Fortuna

As you are looking,

Draw me the money,

Draw the money to me."

Close your eyes while candles are burning and focus on your wish. Let them extinguish altogether.

Immediate Money Manifestation Spell

Need money fast? Use the Immediate Money Manifestation Spell to attract financial abundance instantly and effectively.

Items Needed:

- Green Candle
- White Candle
- Cinnamon Oil
- Pin

Directions:

Inscribe your name on the white candle and dollar signs on the green candle. Anoint the candles with oil visualizing your wish for money to be drawn to you. Arrange the candles on your altar, shrine or table nine inches apart. After accomplishing this state:

"Money, money comes to me

In abundance three times three.

May I be endowed always be

Draw money to me three times three.

And as my will, so mote it be."

Repeat this each day for nine days. Each time bring the white candle one inch nearer to the green candle. When the candles touch, your spell is completed. Visualize the wealth spilling in from the universe each day. On the ninth day, allow the candle to burn down altogether.

Quick Money Spell

Fast-track your finances. Crafted to boost cash flow and unlock financial opportunities.

Items Needed:

- Cauldron
- Water
- Silver coin

Directions:

During the initial night of the Full Moon, fill your cauldron to the halfway point with water. Drop the coin into your cauldron, position it so that the light from the Moon radiates into the water. Lightly sweep your hands above the surface while declaring:

"Lovely Lady of the Moon

Bring to me my wealth soon.

Fill my hands with silver and gold.

All you can give all I can hold."

Repeat three times. Meditate for a few minutes and pour the water upon the Earth.

Prosperity Candle Flame Ritual

Ignite your financial goals. A powerful tool to enhance wealth and attract prosperity."

Items Needed:

- 1 Gold Candle
- 1 Green Candle

- Pine Incense
- Patchouli Incense
- Several Acorns (or Smooth Stones)
- Paper

Directions:

On the bottom of each candle, carve the rune Fehu ($\vdash$). Position them in candle holders crosswise from each other. Position the patchouli incense up beside the gold candle with the pine next to the green one. Light everything and get the incense smoldering.

Draw a third Fehu symbol on the paper, and put your acorns (or stones) on top.

Allow both candles to burn down until they are completely done, and keep the acorns or stones uncovered on the altar while waiting for some extra money comes your way.

Abundant Wealth Money Jar Spell

Secure your financial future. Perfect for sustained income and growing savings.

Items Needed:

- 5 Coins in Various Denominations (Preferable at least one Silver and one Copper)
- 5 Whole Cloves
- 5 Allspice Seeds
- 5 Kernels of Dried Corn
- 5 Sesame Seeds
- 5 Pieces of Cinnamon Stick
- 5 Peanuts (Unshelled and Unsalted)
- A Small Jar with a Lid

Directions:

While you are filling the jar with your ingredients, declare:

"Silver and spices,

Copper and grain.

I desire to raise,

My financial gain."

Once completed, shake bottle while repeating chant. Place the finished bottle close to where you place your purse, pocketbook or wallet.

Elemental Wealth Enhancement Spell

Harness Earth, Water, Air, and Fire. Balance your energies for optimal wealth creation.

Items Needed:

- 1 Green Candle
- Patchouli Incense
- 2 Shot Glasses (or very Small Bottles)
- Salt
- Water

Directions:

Lighting the incense say:

"The element of air now blows riches towards me."

Lighting the candle say:

"The element of fire now lights my way."

Placing some salt on your tongue say:

"The element of earth now grows my fortune."

After drinking the water say:

"The element of water now cleanses me today."

Add water to one shot glass and salt to the other as you allow the incense and candle to burn out. Leave the candle stub, incense ash and shot glasses of both salt and water. Refill the water as needed. Leave on your altar until your money concerns are over.

Prosperity and Wealth Amplification Spell

Maximize your financial potential. Designed to multiply riches and enhance wealth.

Items Needed:

- 9 White Candles
- 6 Green Candles
- 1 Gold Candle
- Pine Oil
- Salt

Directions:

The spell is to start at a minute after midnight on the evening of a cross-quarter day which is April 30 (May 1- Beltane), July 31 (Aug 1-Lammas), Oct 31 (Nov. Samhain1-) and Jan 31 (Feb 1-Imbolc).

All candles should be dressed with pine oil. Arrange your candles with the gold candle placed in the center. The green candles will form a ring around the gold candle. The outermost ring will be the white candles around green candles.

At a minute past midnight on your chosen day, sketch a salt ring around the white circle of candles. Begin by lighting the gold candle first. Moving clockwise, light the green candles, followed by the white candles.

Go around your altar three times, reciting:

"Orbiting Jupiter,

Three times the sun.

Draw to me money,

On the run."

Perform the chant three times. Sit quietly for at least fifteen minutes, envisioning your monetary desires.

Snuff the candles in reverse order.

Candle of Abundance Ritual

Illuminate your path to wealth with the Candle of Abundance Ritual. Burn this candle to unlock continuous financial growth.

Items Needed:

- 1 Green Candle
- Cinnamon Oil
- Vanilla Oil or Extract
- 1 Large Denomination Coin

Directions:

The energy of the flame will help draw new financial opportunities to you. Using something sharp to carve the word "WEALTH" along the side of the candle and then dress the word in the cinnamon and vanilla. Put the coin in the bottom of your candle holder, set the candle in over top. Ignite the candle and let it burn down altogether.

When the candle is finished, leave the wax-covered coin in a safe place to help bring in money to your life.

Abundance Check Manifestation

Write your way to wealth with the Abundance Check Manifestation. A proven method to attract monetary gains through visualization.

Items Needed:

- Blank Check (or a Fake One)
- Green Pen
- Money Drawing Oil

Directions:

Within 24 hours after the New Moon, take a blank check (or one you made). Write your name in the **"Pay to the Order Of"** line. In the box that is on the same line, write **"Paid in Full."** Underneath your name where you would actually write out the dollar amount, write **"Paid in Full."** Sign the check with the words, **"Law of Abundance."**

You could leave that date blank or you can write a specific date that you feel you will believe the amount will come to you.

Ever-Growing Wealth Spell

Plant the seeds of prosperity with the Ever-Growing Wealth Spell. Foster financial growth and watch your assets flourish.

Items Needed:

- Thriving Houseplant

- A Coin
- Dried Patchouli

Directions:

Any plant will do, but a basil plant works better. Just dust a little bit of the patchouli on the soil, then insert the tip of the coin into the soil in the same place so part of the coin is still sticking up out of the dirt. When new money appears in your life, spend the coin right away and put a new one in its place.

Fortune Filling Money Jar Ritual

Secure continuous financial growth with the Fortune Filling Money Jar Ritual. Ideal for building wealth steadily and effectively."

Items Needed:

- 7 Dimes
- Small Jar with Lid (I'd suggest making an opening)
- Bay Leaf
- Paper
- Pen

Directions:

Print your desire on the paper and slip it into the jar. Take the seven dimes in your powerful hand and deposit them one at a time into the jar. As you release each, envision it expanding into massive sums and declare:

"Toward this request, my money grows,

Through leaps and through bounds.

I see the money overflows.

Coins which jingle, coins which shine,

Move toward me now, for you are mine."

Take the bay leaf and print your name on it and drop into the jar. Seal the jar place it where you alone can look at it every day, and where it is not obvious to anybody who comes in your home. Add a couple of coins to the jar each day. The money will stream to you from unanticipated sources. After you receive the money you need, praise your Goddess, Deity etc., for what you've gained. Remove the paper from the jar and bury the paper outside.

Candlelit Wealth Attraction Spell

Brighten your financial path. Light this candle to draw in abundance and prosperity.

Items Needed:

- 2 Black Candles
- Cinnamon Oil
- Pin

Directions:

Begin this spell on Sunday (the Sun), Thursday (Jupiter), or Friday (Venus). Inscribe your name and the words "money", "riches", "wealth", "prosperity" and any other words of strength along the sides of the candles. Light the candles and grip them tightly in your hands until you feel your pulse throbbing beneath your fingers. Recite:

"Bring me riches and wealth.

Bring me silver and gold.

Bring me dollars and coins,

All I can hold."

After ten minutes, extinguish candles. Repeat every night until they are thoroughly burned down.

Romanian Prosperity Charm

Tap into ancient secrets with the Romanian Prosperity Charm. A powerful spell to enhance financial influx and secure riches.

Items Needed:

- Small Bowl
- Three Coins

Directions:

Put the bowl in a place you will look at it every day. Holding the three coins in your powerful hand, declare:

"Trinka five, Trinka five,

Ancient spirits come alive.

Trinka five, Trinka five,

Money grows and money thrives.

Trinka five, Trinka five,

Spirits of Trinka five."

Place the coins into the bowl. Repeat this spell daily, placing the three coins in the bowl each day for nine days. After the nine days, go on performing the spell once a week until you have the money you need.

Wiccan Wealth Booster Spell

Empower your economic status with the Wiccan Wealth Booster Spell. Crafted using traditional Wiccan rites to maximize money flow.

Items Needed:

- 1 Gold Chain
- 1 Gold Ring
- 3 Yellow Candles

Directions:

Cast your circle of protection. Put the yellow candles in front of you, creating a triangle. Light the candles then place the gold ring and the gold chain in the middle of that triangle. Visualize the center of the triangle filling with prosperous energy, with all the abundance of the universe. Visualize as intensely as you can, and then chant the following verse three times:

"Wealth, abundance, prosperity,

Flow now into my life.

Here, now, set me free.

And as my will; so mote it be."

Place the gold ring onto the gold chain. Wear the chain around your neck, feeling the prosperous energy connecting with your own. Wear the gold chain as regularly as you can, so it may draw money into your life.

Creating a Wealth Altar

Creating a wealth altar is a spiritual practice that involves setting up a dedicated space in your home or office where you can focus your intentions on attracting monetary success. By acting as a physical representation of your desires and intentions, this altar becomes a central point for your financial aspirations. By channeling your energy and thoughts towards the altar, you can enhance your ability to attract wealth into your life. Here are detailed steps on how to create a wealth altar that resonates with financial success and personal abundance.

Choosing the Location

The first step in creating a wealth altar is selecting an appropriate location. It should be a quiet, undisturbed area where you can sit comfortably and reflect or meditate. Whether it's a corner in your bedroom, a spot in your living room, or a tiny space in your office, it can work. The key is to choose a spot that feels positive and where you are least likely to be interrupted.

Cleansing the Space

Before setting up your altar, it is essential to cleanse the space to clear out any negative energies and create a conducive environment for your intentions. To purify the area, burn sage or Palo Santo, or use a bell or singing bowl to cleanse with sound. This process helps reset the energy and make the space sacred for your purpose.

Setting the Altar

The altar itself can be a small table, a shelf on the wall, or any flat surface where you can place items that symbolize wealth and success. Cover the altar with a cloth that attracts prosperity —green and gold are colors traditionally associated with abundance and wealth.

Choosing Symbols of Wealth

Select items that represent wealth specifically for you. These can include:

- **Currency:** Actual money, such as coins or bills, particularly in higher denominations or from various countries, if your work has a global focus.
- **Crystals:** Certain crystals, such as citrine, jade, or pyrite, are believed to attract wealth. Place these crystals on your altar to enhance the energy of abundance.
- **Figurines:** Small statues of deities or symbols that represent prosperity, such as Lakshmi, the Hindu goddess of wealth, or a laughing Buddha.
- **Plants:** Adding a plant like a jade or money tree can bring life and a continuous growth energy to your altar.
- **Candles:** Green candles can symbolize the growth of your wealth, while gold candles can represent the accumulation of money.

Adding Personal Items

It's also beneficial to include personal items that represent your goals or aspirations. Whether it's a business card or a dream purchase, select something that reflects your personal definition of success.

Activating the Altar

Once your altar is set up, activate it by spending time in front of it each day. There are three options: lighting the candles, holding the crystals, or visualizing your financial goals as already attained. Speak affirmations aloud, such as "I attract wealth naturally" or "My actions create constant prosperity."

Regular Maintenance

Keeping your wealth altar clean is essential for its maintenance. Regularly change out the items as your goals grow or as you feel drawn to add new items. Maintain a refreshed energy by periodically re-cleansing the space and reaffirming your intentions.

By constructing and sustaining a money shrine, you are committing a physical location to your financial goals, which can channel your energies and intentions towards accomplishing monetary prosperity. This practice not only enhances your spiritual connection to wealth but also serves as a daily reminder of your financial goals, reinforcing your commitment to achieving them.

5

MASTERING MINDSET

The Law of Attraction suggests that positive thoughts can lead to positive experiences, while negative thoughts can bring negative experiences. This concept, currently trending in personal development and spiritual growth, underscores the mind's role in shaping our financial circumstances. When applied to financial aspirations, the Law of Attraction transforms and fosters an initiative towards wealth creation.

The Basics of the Law of Attraction

The foundational principle of the Law of Attraction is that "like attracts like." This means that by focusing your thoughts on positive outcomes, you are more likely to attract similar positive experiences and opportunities. Focusing on negative thoughts could bring about more negativity and obstacles. With finance, this principle implies that staying focused on prosperity increases the chances of attracting financial opportunities and success.

Manifesting Financial Success

If you want financial success using the Law of Attraction, it's important to define your financial goals clearly. Whether it's achieving a certain income level, saving a specific amount of money, or eliminating debt, clarity is critical. Once you've determined these goals, the next step is to coordinate your thoughts, emotions, and energies with them. Visualization is a powerful tool in this process. Visualizing achieving your financial goals regularly strengthens your actions towards achieving them.

Affirmations and Positive Thinking

Affirmations are statements that, when repeated, boost confidence in one's abilities and aspirations. Affirmations in finance can comprise statements like "I can achieve financial prosperity" or "I am drawing in many sources of income."

Emotional Alignment and Belief Systems

One of the less obvious elements of the Law of Attraction is how your emotions are influenced by thoughts and beliefs. Emotions are powerful indicators of what your subconscious indeed expects. Feeling anxious or doubtful about your financial goals could show negative beliefs about money that may impede your journey to wealth. To effectively apply the Law of Attraction, it's crucial to address and rectify these negative emotions and beliefs, replacing them with positive ones that align with financial abundance.

Taking Action

Thoughts, emotions, and action all play essential roles in the Law of Attraction. The universe is more likely to present opportunities when you are actively seeking them and working toward your goals. Some actions you can take are educating yourself about investments, networking for new business opportunities, or managing your money wisely. Such actions show a readiness to receive and handle the wealth you're attracting.

Sustaining Focus

Focusing on your financial intentions is essential for the Law of Attraction to work effectively. Daily practices such as meditation, keeping a journal of financial goals and progress, and setting aside regular times for visualization exercises can support this. These practices ensure that your financial aspirations remain a priority, attracting the positive energies required to make them a reality.

Understanding can affect your financial reality and applying the Law of Attraction. It involves more than wishful thinking—it requires a committed approach to aligning thoughts, emotions, and actions with your financial goals. By fostering a positive mindset, challenging limiting beliefs, and pursuing your financial goals, you can use the Law of Attraction to build a prosperous future.

Techniques for Maintaining Positive Financial Thoughts

Maintaining a positive financial mindset is critical for attaining and preserving wealth. However, staying optimistic about finances can be challenging, especially in the face of setbacks or economic uncertainty. Practicing practical techniques to foster positive financial thoughts can greatly affect your financial well-being and overall happiness. Here are several strategies designed to help foster a consistently positive perspective on economic matters.

Visualization Techniques

Using visualization can be a powerful technique for staying positive about finances. It involves creating vivid, detailed mental images of achieving your financial goals. This practice not only reinforces a positive financial outlook, but also activates the subconscious mind to notice and pursue overlooked opportunities. Dedicate a few minutes daily to visualize achieving your financial goals, like buying a home or building a successful business. This positive mental rehearsal can boost your confidence and motivation.

Affirmations

Positive affirmations can transform negative thoughts into positive ones when repeated regularly. Develop a set of financial affirmations that resonate with your specific goals and repeat them daily. Using affirmations like "I trust my skills in managing my finances prudently" or "I am manifesting financial abundance in my life" can help shift your mindset from scarcity to abundance.

Financial Journaling

A financial journal is an effective tool for fostering a positive economic mindset. Regularly write your financial successes, no matter how small, and reflect on the progress you've made toward your goals. By practicing this habit, you can gain a more balanced perspective on your financial journey, focusing on your accomplishments instead of what you haven't achieved. Enhance feelings of control and optimism by utilizing the journal for goal planning and financial tracking.

Educate Yourself

Financial literacy is critical to maintaining a positive economic outlook. Learning about the ins and outs of money, including earning, saving, investing, and spending wisely, can reduce anxiety and build confidence. Make an investment of time in reading books, attending workshops, and researching articles on personal finance. Knowledge is power, and being well-informed enables you to decide with greater confidence and peace of mind.

Set Realistic Financial Goals

Maintaining positivity requires setting achievable, realistic financial goals. Unrealistic goals can lead to frustration and setbacks, which may dampen your financial outlook. Break down larger goals into smaller, manageable steps and acknowledge each milestone you accomplish. This approach not only makes the process more manageable but also provides frequent opportunities for positive reinforcement.

Practice Gratitude

When it comes to finance, gratitude entails recognizing and valuing what you already possess, rather than solely longing for more. Start or finish each day by reflecting on at least three financial elements you are thankful for, like a secure income, the opportunity to save, or the valuable knowledge gained from past financial missteps. This practice can shift your focus from scarcity to abundance, encouraging a healthier relationship with money.

Mindfulness and Meditation

Mindfulness meditation has been found to be a useful tool in dealing with stress and anxiety related to financial issues. Regular practice helps you stay present and grounded, preventing worry about future economic uncertainties. Practicing mindfulness helps people become more aware of impulsive spending, allowing them to make better financial choices.

Connect with Positive Influences

Being around people who have a positive attitude towards money can affect your financial mindset. Positive financial role models can provide practical advice, support, and motivation to cultivate and maintain a prosperous mindset.

By integrating these methods into your everyday routine, you can develop and maintain a positive financial mindset, leading to greater financial achievements and a more satisfying life. These practices help you take control of your financial future with confidence and optimism by actively managing your finances.

Success Stories

Positive thinking has proven to be a reality, not just a motivational idea, for many successful people in transforming their financial destinies. Overcoming substantial financial obstacles and achieving remarkable success is possible for several entrepreneurs, investors, and ordinary individuals who maintain a positive mindset. These real-life examples show the powerful impact of positive thinking on financial outcomes.

Chris Gardner: From Homelessness to Millionaire

The story of Chris Gardner, depicted in *The Pursuit of Happyness*, shows how positive thinking can bring about significant financial transformation. Gardner, once homeless and struggling as a single father, never let his dire circumstances crush his spirits. He continued to believe in his potential and maintained a relentless pursuit of his career goals. His perseverance and optimistic mindset finally paid off when he landed a job as a stockbroker, propelling him towards millionaire status. Gardner's journey underscores the power of optimism and perseverance in overcoming financial and personal adversity.

John Paul DeJoria: From Living in a Car to Billionaire

The co-founder of Paul Mitchell and Patron, John Paul DeJoria, had a past where he lived in a car and sold shampoo door-to-door. Despite his initial struggles, DeJoria always believed that better days were ahead. His attention was on finding solutions instead of fixating on problems, and he consistently sought opportunities to enhance his circumstances. His positive mindset helped him identify potential in the beauty industry, leading to the creation of a multi-billion dollar empire. DeJoria's success is evidence that having a positive mindset can pave the way for incredible financial prospects.

Daymond John: From His Mother's Living Room to FUBU Founder

Daymond John, founder of FUBU and a "Shark Tank" star, built his multi-million dollar empire from his mother's living room with only $40. Despite limited resources, John used his positive mindset to see every challenge as an opportunity and every failure as a lesson. His powerful belief in his vision and adaptability resulted in the establishment of a brand that generated over $6 billion in worldwide sales. John's journey highlights the critical role of optimism in navigating the entrepreneurial landscape.

These stories show that positive thinking is a powerful tool for building resilience, creating opportunities, and attaining financial success. Each of these individuals harnessed the power of a positive economic outlook to transform their lives, illustrating that a mindset can indeed influence material outcomes.

6

INNER WEALTH

The correlation between money and happiness is a multifaceted and often disputed matter, interlaced with psychological and spiritual aspects. While conventional wisdom suggests that money can't buy happiness, we must not completely disregard its role in influencing our life satisfaction. Understanding the complex relationship between financial stability, personal wealth, and our well-being is essential.

The Psychological Impact of Money on Happiness

Money mainly impacts happiness by reducing stress related to financial insecurity, as seen from a psychological standpoint. When basic needs are met effortlessly, anxiety and stress decrease, resulting in improved mental health and overall happiness. The happiness obtained from extra wealth diminishes beyond these essentials. The "hedonic treadmill" phenomenon implies that as income increases, so do expectations and desires, leading to a balance in happiness gains.

Research in positive psychology often points to an income threshold after which increased earnings have little effect on life satisfaction. On the other hand, the manner in which individuals spend their money can impact their happiness. Spending money on experiences like travel, learning, or socializing has a more sustainable effect on happiness than purchasing material items. Various studies have indicated that individuals who engage in acts of financial generosity, such as donating money or providing financial assistance to loved ones, experience a heightened sense of joy and fulfillment, highlighting the significance of social bonds in shaping the relationship between wealth and happiness.

Money and Its Spiritual Dimensions

Spiritually, money holds a dual power: it can either enable growth and self-realization or lead to materialism and disconnection. One of the key teachings in various spiritual traditions is to not become overly attached to material wealth. Money is considered a means to promote personal development, support others, and accomplish life objectives that are consistent with one's values and ethics.

For instance, the concept of "right livelihood" in Buddhism emphasizes earning money through means that do not harm others and contribute positively to one's spiritual development. In many Christian teachings, managing wealth in line with spiritual values is seen as a moral obligation that benefits society.

Finding Balance: Money as a Tool for Happiness and Spiritual Fulfillment

To achieve a balance between personal well-being and spiritual enrichment, one must consider practicality and ethics when making financial decisions. It's about recognizing that while money can provide comfort and security, it should not dominate one's values or sense of self-worth.

Developing financial habits that reflect this balanced approach can lead to greater happiness and spiritual depth. Possible steps include creating meaningful financial goals that align with personal values, using money to foster community connections, and making socially responsible and environmentally sustainable investment choices.

Ultimately, how we acquire, use, and attach meaning to money mediates its impact on happiness. Happiness can be achieved by integrating financial wealth with strong relationships, personal growth, and spiritual depth. By approaching money as a tool to enhance not just personal comfort but also to foster human connections and live out one's ethical beliefs, it becomes possible to enjoy the benefits of wealth without falling into the trap of materialism. Money and happiness are interconnected, creating a positive cycle that benefits individuals and communities.

Money anxiety can be a significant source of stress, affecting not only your financial well-being but also your overall health and relationships. Anxiety stemming from financial worries, such as bill payments and debt, can negatively impact happiness and overall life satisfaction. Fortunately, there are effective techniques to manage and reduce financial stress, helping you regain control and peace of mind.

Understanding the Source of Anxiety

Understanding the root causes is key to conquering money anxiety. This involves taking a close look at your financial situation, identifying specific stressors such as debt, inadequate savings, or lack of income security. Recognizing these problems is essential as it changes your mindset from worrying to finding solutions.

Creating a Financial Plan

Developing a clear financial plan can significantly reduce anxiety by providing a roadmap for addressing financial challenges. This plan should include:

- **Budgeting:** Track your income and expenses to understand where your money goes each month. Take advantage of budgeting apps or spreadsheets to organize and oversee your financial situation.
- **Setting Financial Goals:** Define short-term and long-term financial goals that are realistic and achievable. Setting specific goals for saving, debt repayment, or retirement planning can boost motivation and alleviate uncertainty.
- **Debt Management Strategy:** If debt is a major source of anxiety, outline a plan to pay it off. Look into approaches like the debt snowball or avalanche techniques, aimed at strategically paying down debts.

Establishing an Emergency Fund

One of the most effective ways to mitigate financial anxiety is by building an emergency fund. Having a financial safety net can bring peace of mind in case of unexpected expenses. Start small, aiming to save a few months' worth of living expenses. Having a modest emergency fund can offer financial stability and make you feel more confident.

Mindfulness and Relaxation Techniques

Mindfulness and relaxation techniques can be powerful tools for managing anxiety of any kind, including financial anxiety.

Engaging in practices like meditation, deep breathing exercises, or yoga can bring calmness to your mind and decrease stress. By learning to stay present and engaged in the moment, you can prevent financial worries from overwhelming you.

Seeking Professional Help

It can be tough to handle financial anxiety by yourself. In such cases, seeking help from a financial advisor or a counselor specializing in financial therapy can be beneficial. These professionals specialize in providing expert advice on finance management and aiding in the development of anxiety coping strategies.

Educate Yourself About Finances

Lack of knowledge about finances can exacerbate anxiety. Increase your confidence and reduce fears by educating yourself on financial concepts, investment options, and economic trends. Many community colleges, libraries, and online platforms offer courses on personal finance and investing.

Communicating Openly About Finances

If money anxiety affects your relationships, it's important to communicate openly with your partner, family, or close friends. Talking about financial matters can offer both emotional support and practical solutions or fresh ideas for better managing finances as a team.

Regular Financial Reviews

By regularly evaluating your financial situation, you can ensure you're on the right path and make any necessary plan modifications. Plan a monthly or quarterly review to gauge your progress towards financial goals and tackle any other sources of worry. Engaging in this habit helps you stay proactive and connected to your financial well-being.

By implementing these strategies, you can address the underlying causes of your financial anxiety, develop a healthier relationship with money, and achieve a greater sense of financial stability and peace of mind.

Balancing material and spiritual wealth is a nuanced endeavor that requires intentional effort to align one's financial pursuits with deeper spiritual values. Finding balance between material success and other aspects creates a more fulfilling life. Learn how to integrate material ambitions and spiritual growth, giving equal importance to both dimensions.

Defining Material and Spiritual Wealth

Material wealth usually includes physical assets, money, and possessions that contribute to someone's financial stability and comfort. Spiritual wealth, on the other hand, relates to intangible qualities such as inner peace, ethical integrity, personal fulfillment, and the quality of relationships. It involves a strong sense of connection to something larger than oneself, whether that's through religion, philosophy, or community.

Setting Intentional Goals

To achieve a balance between material and spiritual wealth, start by defining success in both areas. This involves setting goals that not only consider financial targets but also how these pursuits align with your personal values and spiritual beliefs. One way to fulfill material needs and spiritual aspirations is by earning money through a profession that has a positive impact on society, like for instance.

Mindful Consumption

It's easy to get caught up in excessive consumerism while chasing material wealth. Mindful consumption involves making purchasing decisions that are intentional and aligned with one's values, which supports both financial health and spiritual well-being. This method promotes questioning such as, "Is this really necessary?"", "How does this purchase impact the environment?", and "Is this aligned with my spiritual values?" Mindful consumption not only helps in managing financial resources wisely but also in living a life that reflects one's ethical beliefs.

Spiritual Practices that Encourage Detachment

Spiritual traditions often stress detachment from material possessions for spiritual development. By practicing activities such as meditation, prayer, or contemplative reflection, one can develop a mindset where happiness and contentment are not solely reliant on material success. These practices encourage a focus on the present moment and foster an appreciation for life's non-material aspects.

Generosity and Giving

The most effective way to achieve a balance between material and spiritual wealth is through practicing generosity. Giving to others, whether in the form of charity, time, or resources, can diminish the hold that material desires have on one's life. It also provides a profound sense of connection and purpose, key components of spiritual wealth. In addition, many people observe that this act of giving generates a cycle of abundance that comes back to them in various ways, improving both material and spiritual well-being.

Integrating Work and Personal Beliefs

Choosing a career or business ventures that resonate with your personal beliefs can greatly contribute to a balanced life. Aligning work with one's spiritual values not only brings material wealth but also enriches a sense of meaning and purpose, enhancing spiritual wealth.

Regular Reflection and Adjustment

To maintain a balance between material and spiritual wealth, it is important to constantly reflect and make adjustments. Regularly assessing how well your financial and lifestyle choices align with your spiritual goals can help you make necessary adjustments. It could involve adjusting your schedule, reallocating resources, or changing career paths to improve your well-being.

Balancing material and spiritual wealth is not about choosing one over the other but about finding ways to integrate both into a cohesive and fulfilling life. By setting deliberate objectives, adopting mindful consumption habits, and aligning professional pursuits with personal values, individuals can ensure that their quest for material prosperity doesn't hinder their spiritual development. This holistic approach to life invites a deeper satisfaction and a richer, more meaningful existence.

CONCLUSION

It's not a matter of choosing between material and spiritual wealth, but of harmonizing them for a fulfilling life. By setting deliberate goals, engaging in mindful consumption, and aligning professional pursuits with personal values, individuals can safeguard their spiritual growth while seeking material wealth. This holistic approach to life invites a more profound satisfaction and a more prosperous, more meaningful existence.

Final Thoughts on Money Magic

As we conclude our exploration of *Abundance Spells*, it's crucial to reflect on the profound connections between our financial behaviors and broader spiritual and emotional well-being. This book explores different realms, from practical to mystical, showing that money is more than just a means for acquiring things but a force that connects with our personal energies and beliefs.

Integrating the practices discussed in *Abundance Spells* into your daily life can transform your approach to personal finance. Align your financial actions with spiritual values through techniques like creating a wealth altar and casting Wiccan spells. The book also emphasizes the importance of a balanced perspective—recognizing that true wealth encompasses both material success and spiritual fulfillment.

When moving ahead, blend mindful budgeting and strategic investments with spiritual practices that resonate, like meditation, affirmations, or ethical financial decisions. Remember, the goal is not just to accumulate wealth but to create a harmonious and abundant life.

Let *Abundance Spells* be a guide to rethinking how you interact with money, encouraging you not only to seek financial success but also to cultivate a life rich in spiritual health. When you combine these elements, you begin a journey towards not only financial freedom but also a fulfilling and well-rounded prosperity.

Continuing Your Journey

As you embark on a journey of financial spirituality, integrating the principles of *Abundance Spells* into your life, the path doesn't end on the last page of the book. In fact, it's just the start of delving deeper into the connection between your financial habits and your spiritual principles. Continuing this journey involves constant learning, training, and growth. Here are some tips for further exploration and enriching your understanding and application of financial spirituality.

Expand Your Learning

Education is a lifelong process, and expanding your knowledge about both finance and spirituality can enhance your ability to integrate these areas effectively. You should explore books, workshops, and courses on personal finance, ethical investing, and spiritual practices for wealth. Authors like Deepak Chopra and Suze Orman blend financial advice with spiritual insight, offering a holistic approach to money management.

Practice Mindfulness and Meditation

Mindfulness and meditation are foundational practices that can deepen your connection to both your financial and spiritual goals. Regular meditation fosters clear thinking, reduces stress, and enhances focus, all of which contribute to making wise financial choices. Mindfulness in spending and investing can also lead to more intentional and fulfilling financial choices.

Join Communities

Finding a community of like-minded individuals can be incredibly supportive as you delve deeper into financial spirituality. Seek out local or online groups centered around holistic financial well-being, ethical investing, or integrating spirituality into daily life. Such communities can offer support, accountability, and new perspectives. Taking part in discussions and sharing experiences can also provide motivation and inspiration.

Keep a Journal

Keep a journal solely for documenting your financial spiritual journey. Regular entries can help you track your progress, reflect on your learning, and document insights from your spiritual practices. This journal can be a valuable tool for observing how your financial decisions align with your spiritual growth. Reflect on both successes and areas for improvement.

Engage with Financial Advisors

To manage your wealth in line with your spiritual beliefs, seek advice from financial advisors specializing in ethical investing. These professionals can provide guidance on how to balance financial gain with personal and communal well-being.

Apply Ethical and Socially Responsible Investing

Discover how ethical and socially responsible investing can serve as a practical expression of your financial spirituality. This approach considers the social and environmental consequences of investments. It seeks to contribute to a positive impact on investment dollars. When you align your investments with your values, you seek both financial returns and positive impact on the planet and society.

Teach and Share Your Knowledge

Teaching others what you have learned is a fulfilling way to deepen your understanding. Sharing your journey and insights into financial spirituality can reinforce your own practices and help others find a path that merges their economic and spiritual lives. Blogging, speaking, and informal discussions are powerful ways to teach and inspire others while strengthening your own knowledge.

Reflect and Reassess Regularly

Continual reflection and reassessment of your financial and spiritual goals are crucial as circumstances and priorities change. Make it a habit to regularly review your finances, spiritual alignment, and adjust plans accordingly.

To continue your exploration of financial spirituality, it's important to stay curious, stay involved, and take proactive actions. By adopting these tips, you can be certain that your financial practices not only enhance your material life but also contribute to your spiritual well-being and the greater good of society.

While you explore the enchanting realm of financial magic in this book, remember that each turn of the page is a part of a bigger journey towards not only financial prosperity but also personal and spiritual growth. May the spells and insights shared here illuminate your path and empower you to weave magic into your financial tapestry. Good luck on your transformative journey—may it bring you abundance, fulfillment, and peace. Happy conjuring!

REFERENCES

5 Self-Healing Practices - Bio Spiritual Energy Healing. https://www.biospiritual-energy-healing.com/5-self-healing-practices/

Creating an Effective Home Office. https://loudounbasements.com/creating-an-effective-home-office-with-loudoun-basements/

Discovering Meaning and Purpose: Your Personal Guide | Future Self Journal. https://www.futureselfjournal.com/blogs/blog/discovering-meaning-and-purpose-your-personal-guide

Empowering Your Career Journey: A Guide to Christian Career Coaching - Online Mental Health Reviews. https://onlinementalhealthreviews.com/empowering-your-career-journey-a-guide-to-christian-career-coaching/

Introduction to Credit Card Debt - Personal Finance Blog - Best Finance Care. https://www.bestfinancecare.com/introduction-credit-card-debt/

Recharge and Thrive: 5 Steps to Embrace Self-Care for a Balanced Life. https://www.thegratitudemethod.com/post/recharge-and-thrive-5-steps-to-embrace-self-care-for-a-balanced-life

Unleashing the Power of PEMF Therapy: Exploring its Health Benefits | Almagia. https://almagia.com/unleashing-the-power-of-pemf-therapy-exploring-its-health-benefits/

What's an Intuitive Personality?. https://www.al-hamdoulillah.com/blog/developpement-personnel/whats-an-intuitive-personality.html

ABOUT THE AUTHOR

Monique Joiner Siedlak is a writer, witch, and warrior on a mission to awaken people to their greatest potential through the power of storytelling infused with mysticism, modern paganism, and new age spirituality. At the young age of 12, she began rigorously studying the fascinating philosophy of Wicca. By the time she was 20, she was self-initiated into the craft, and hasn't looked back ever since. To this day, she has authored over 40 books pertaining to the magick and mysteries of life.

To find out more about Monique Joiner Siedlak artistically, spiritually, and personally, feel free to visit her **official website**.

www.mojosiedlak.com

- facebook.com/mojosiedlak
- x.com/mojosiedlak
- instagram.com/mojosiedlak
- pinterest.com/mojosiedlak
- bookbub.com/authors/monique-joiner-siedlak

MORE BOOKS BY MONIQUE

African Spirituality Beliefs and Practices

Hoodoo

Seven African Powers: The Orishas

Cooking for the Orishas

Lucumi: The Ways of Santeria

Voodoo of Louisiana

Haitian Vodou

Orishas of Trinidad

Connecting with your Ancestors

Blood Magick

The Orishas

Vodun: West Africa's Spiritual Life

Marie Laveau: Life of a Voodoo Queen

Candomblé: Dancing for the God

Umbanda

Exploring the Rich and Diverse World

Divination Magic for Beginners

Divination with Runes

Divination with Diloggún

Divination with Osteomancy

Divination with the Tarot

Divination with Stones

The Beginner's Guide to Inner Growth

Astral Projection for Beginners

Meditation for Beginners

Reiki for Beginners

Mastering Your Inner Potential

Creative Visualization

Manifesting With the Law of Attraction

Holistic Healing and Energy

Healing Animals with Reiki

Crystal Healing

Communicating with Your Spirit Guides

Empathic Understanding and Enlightenment

Being an Empath Today

Life on Fire

Healing Your Inner Child

Change Your Life

Raising Your Vibe

The Indie Author's Guides

The Indie Author's Guide to Fast Drafting Your Novel

Get a Handle on Life

Get a Handle on Stress

Time Bound

Get a Handle on Anxiety

Get a Handle on Depression

Get a Handle on Procrastination

The Holistic Yoga and Wellness Series

Yoga for Beginners

Yoga for Stress

Yoga for Back Pain

Yoga for Weight Loss

Yoga for Flexibility

Yoga for Advanced Beginners

Yoga for Fitness

Yoga for Runners

Yoga for Energy

Yoga for Your Sex Life

Yoga to Beat Depression and Anxiety

Yoga for Menstruation

Yoga to Detox Your Body

Yoga to Tone Your Body

The DIY Body Care Series

Creating Your Own Body Butter

Creating Your Own Body Scrub

Creating Your Own Body Spray

WANT TO BE
FIRST TO KNOW?

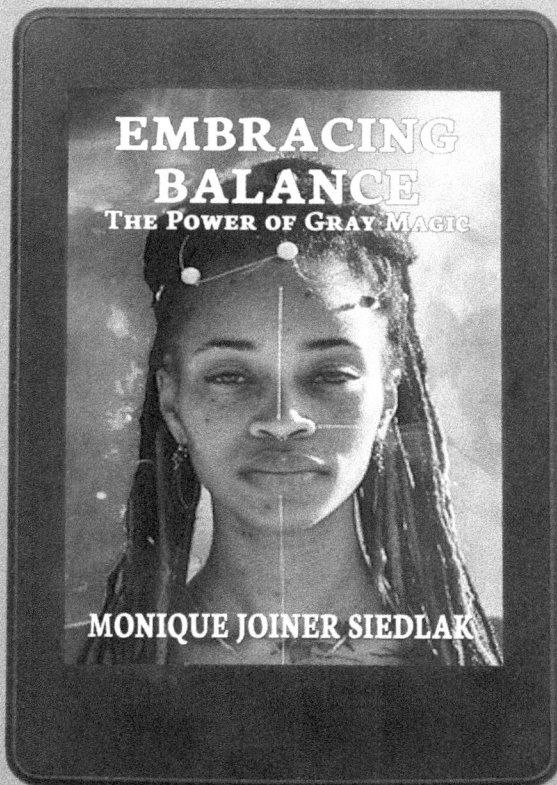

EMBRACING
BALANCE
The Power of Gray Magic

MONIQUE JOINER SIEDLAK

JOIN MY NEWSLETTER!

WWW.MOJOSIEDLAK.COM/MOONLIGHT-MUSINGS

SUPPORT ME BY LEAVING A REVIEW!

goodreads

amazon

BookBub

Download on
Apple Books

GET IT ON
Google Play

nook
by Barnes & Noble

Rakuten
kobo

www.ingramcontent.com/pod-product-compliance
Lightning Source LLC
Chambersburg PA
CBHW071611040426
42452CB00008B/1314